George Washington

BY DARICE BAILER

Published by The Child's World®
1980 Lookout Drive • Mankato, MN 56003-1705
800-599-READ • www.childsworld.com

Acknowledgments
The Child's World®: Mary Swensen, Publishing Director
Red Line Editorial: Editorial direction and production
The Design Lab: Design

Photographs ©: Joe Cicak/iStockphoto, cover, 1; Don Troiani/
Corbis, 4; Lebrecht Music & Arts/Corbis, 7; GeorgiosArt/
iStockphoto, 9; AS400 DB/Corbis, 10; GraphicaArtis/
Corbis, 13; GeorgiosArt/iStock/ThinkStock, 14; Francis G.
Mayer/Corbis, 17; Junius Brutus Stearns/AS400 DB/Corbis,
18; AP Images, 21

ISBN 9781503808553
LCCN 2015958436

Printed in the United States of America
Mankato, MN
June, 2016
PA02303

ABOUT THE AUTHOR

Darice Bailer is the author of many books for young readers, including biographies for The World's Greatest Artists series for The Child's World®, which were 2014 Junior Library Guild Selections for the Series Nonfiction Level: Social Studies. Her book *Measuring Temperature* was also a 2014 Junior Library Guild Selection for science. She lives in Connecticut with her family.

Table of Contents

Washington led soldiers into the Battle of Trenton in 1776.

CHAPTER ONE

A Surprise Attack

George Washington sat on his horse. It was Christmas afternoon in 1776. Washington was the **commander** of the American army. The King of England ruled the American **colonies**. He had the strongest army in the world. But now, Americans were fighting for their freedom.

Washington planned to march all night. He was headed to Trenton, New Jersey. The British troops were camped there. Washington wanted to surprise them before they woke up. It was very cold and growing dark.

Washington's men shivered in the snow. Some of his soldiers were barefoot. Their bloody feet left tracks in the snow. A few men wore blankets to keep warm.

That night, it rained, hailed, and snowed. Sleet stung Washington's face. Ahead, he saw the Delaware River. Washington asked his men to keep boats there. He climbed aboard one of the boats. He stood at the front. The soldiers rowed past blocks of ice.

They reached the other side of the river. Washington climbed on his horse. The men were half frozen. Some were sick. Washington told them to press on.

Cold rain turned the snow on the ground to ice. The weather was terrible. Washington's horse tried to climb a hill. Its hooves skidded. Washington needed to continue. The country's freedom was in his hands. Washington's horse finally made it up the hill.

Washington crossed the Delaware
River with 2,400 soldiers.

The soldiers stumbled through the storm all night. If they stopped to rest, they would die. In the morning, Washington saw the enemy camps. He rushed toward them on his horse. Washington charged ahead of his soldiers. He was the first one through the snow.

Washington's troops surprised the tired British soldiers. The Americans won the battle. Washington was a hero. He bravely led the troops. One day, he would lead a country.

Washington was named commander of the
American army on June 19, 1775.

Washington created more than 90 maps in his lifetime.

CHAPTER TWO

A Leader on the Frontier

George was born on February 22, 1732. He had reddish hair and gray-blue eyes. He grew up on a farm in Virginia. Virginia was one of 13 colonies. They were ruled by Great Britain. George's older brother fought in the British army. George wanted to be a soldier, too.

When George was 11, his father died. George learned to read and write in school. But his mother wasn't rich. She couldn't send him to college.

So George got a job as a **surveyor**. He was 17 years old. Virginia was covered with forests. His job was to measure the land and create maps.

Washington grew to be more than six feet tall. He was strong and muscular. The **governor** of Virginia gave him a job. Washington was 21 years old. Great Britain owned land along the Ohio River. But France said they owned that land, too. Washington's job was to give a message. It was to tell the French to leave. It was a very risky task.

Washington rode hundreds of miles. He led his horse through ice-cold rivers. Along the way, he met Native Americans. Washington had seen some of the **frontier** before. Now, he got to know it even better. Washington gave the French the message. But they would not leave. Washington headed back home.

The disagreement with France grew into a war.
It was called the French and Indian War.

He told the governor the French wouldn't move. The governor was not happy. He asked if Washington would help fight the French. Washington said yes.

On July 9, 1755, Washington rode into battle. The fight was deadly. It was during the French and Indian War. The French and Native Americans had teamed up. They fired their guns from the woods.

Washington's horse was shot and killed. Four bullets hit Washington. They tore through his hat and uniform. But he wasn't hurt.

Washington learned many lessons during the war. It ended eight years later. He learned how to fight in the woods. He also learned how to lead.

Martha Custis only knew George Washington for a couple of months before they got married.

CHAPTER THREE

War Lessons

In 1759, Washington married Martha Custis. Martha's husband had died. She had two children. Washington moved his new family to his home. It was called Mount Vernon. He was content.

Then, trouble started. Great Britain was out of money. They spent too much of it on wars. They taxed the **colonists** to pay for it. Many colonists, including Washington, didn't think the taxes were fair. In April 1775, the colonists had enough. They fought against British troops near Boston. It was the beginning of the Revolutionary War. Washington met with colony leaders in Massachusetts. They needed an army leader. They chose Washington to lead the fight against the British. He was already a war hero.

On July 4, 1776, the colonies claimed **independence**. This made the British government mad. The British sent 33,000 soldiers and sailors to the colonies. Many poor farm boys joined Washington. Most were 15 to 25 years old. They wanted to fight for their freedom. But the new country didn't have money. It couldn't feed or clothe its soldiers. The men had little food. They were dressed in rags.

The war didn't go well. The British attacked New York in August 1776. Washington's soldiers were scared and ran. Washington pulled back. In November 1776, the British surrounded colonial soldiers. They captured approximately 3,000 men.

Washington fought at the Battle of Princeton in 1777.

In the summer of 1780, help came. Approximately 6,000 French soldiers sailed into Rhode Island. They came to aid the colonists. They gave the soldiers guns. The French trained the colonists to shoot. On October 19, 1781, Washington conquered the British. It was the last battle of the war. Two years later, the two sides made peace. The colonists won the war. They now lived in an independent country.

Washington joined other leaders in Philadelphia to discuss the new constitution.

CHAPTER FOUR

The First President

America was finally free. Washington joined the leaders from the other states. They met in Philadelphia. Together they wrote the **constitution**. It explained how the government would work. The United States would have a president. The president would be **elected** every four years. In 1789, the country picked its first president. It was Washington.

Washington was 57 years old. He was old and tired. He didn't want to lead. But his country needed him. So he agreed.

The nation's first capital was New York City. Washington rode through the capital. It was April 30, 1789. Church bells rang through town. More than 10,000 people were there. Many stood in the street or on rooftops. Washington went to the Federal Hall. He took the oath of office. He became the first president of the nation. The crowds cheered.

A new capital would be built. It would be named after Washington. Washington chose to have a home built for all presidents. It would later be called the White House. But Washington never got to live there.

Washington served two **terms** as president. He helped develop the young country. When he retired, he returned to Mount Vernon. One day, he rode his horse around his farm. First it snowed, then a cold rain fell. Washington got very sick from the cold. Two

Washington gave his first presidential speech on April 30, 1789.

days later, on December 14, 1799, he died. He was 67 years old.

Washington led an army and a nation. And he became the father of a country.

1730

←— **February 22, 1732** George Washington is born in Virginia.

←— **April 12, 1743** Washington's father dies.

←— **July 1749** Washington becomes a surveyor for Virginia.

←—**1752** Washington joins the Virginia army.

←— **October 31, 1753** The governor of Virginia asks Washington to deliver a message to the French.

←—**1754-1758** Washington fights for the British in the French and Indian War.

←— **January 6, 1759** Washington marries Martha Custis.

←— **June 19, 1775** Washington becomes commander of the American army.

←— **October 19, 1781** Washington defeats the British at Yorktown, Virginia.

←— **April 30, 1789** Washington is elected the first president of the United States.

←— **February 13, 1793** Washington is elected president for a second term.

←— **December 14, 1799** Washington dies at Mount Vernon.

1800

colonies (KOL-uh-nees) Colonies are large areas of land that are ruled by another country. King George III ruled the 13 colonies.

colonists (KOL-uh-nists) Colonists are people who live on land that is starting to be settled. Great Britain taxed the American colonists.

commander (kuh-MAN-der) A commander is a leader of an army or base. As commander, Washington led his men in battle.

constitution (kon-stuh-TOO-shun) The laws and beliefs of a country are written in its constitution. The U.S. Constitution says that the United States selects a president every four years.

elected (ih-LEK-tid) Elected means chosen by a vote. Washington was elected the first president of the United States.

frontier (frun-TEER) The frontier is the land at the farthest edge of a settled area. Washington met Native Americans on the frontier.

governor (GUV-uh-ner) A governor is the head of a state or colony. Washington told the governor of Virginia about his meeting with the French.

independence (in-di-PEN-duns) Independence is freedom from outside control. Washington helped the country win its independence.

surveyor (sur-VAY-er) A surveyor is someone who explores and measures land. Washington hiked through the woods when he was a surveyor.

terms (TERMS) Terms are periods of time an official serves in office. Washington served two terms as president.

In the Library

Collard, Sneed B. III. *George Washington: Our First President.*
New York: Marshall Cavendish Benchmark, 2010.

Keating, Frank. *George: George Washington, Our Founding Father.*
New York: Simon & Schuster Books for Young Readers, 2012.

Rockwell, Anne. *Big George: How a Shy Boy Became
President Washington.* Orlando: Harcourt, 2009.

On the Web

Visit our Web site for links about
George Washington: **childsworld.com/links**

*Note to Parents, Teachers, and Librarians: We routinely verify our Web links to make
sure they are safe and active sites. So encourage your readers to check them out!*

INDEX